Let's Read the Lost Sheep Story

For Lucie A.A.

Text by Lois Rock
Illustrations copyright © 2000 Alex Ayliffe
This edition copyright © 2004 Lion Hudson

The moral rights of the author and illustrator
have been asserted

A Lion Children's Book
an imprint of
Lion Hudson plc
Mayfield House, 256 Banbury Road,
Oxford OX2 7DH, England
www.lionhudson.com
ISBN 0 7459 4932 0

First edition 2004
1 3 5 7 9 10 8 6 4 2 0

A catalogue record for this book is available
from the British Library

Typeset in 32/46 Kidprint MT Bold
Printed and bound in Singapore

**This Bible tale is adapted from Jesus' parable of the Lost Sheep,
which can be found in Luke, chapter 15**

let's read the
Lost Sheep Story

Retold by Lois Rock ✳ Illustrated by Alex Ayliffe

LION
CHILDREN'S

Jesus told this story of a shepherd and his sheep.

A hundred woolly animals
is quite a lot to keep!

Now one of them was mischievous: he thought,

I'll go and hide.

It made him smile to see the shepherd searching far and wide.

Next time he ran,

and ran,

and ran,

then hid behind a stone.

He felt so clever at the way he'd gone off on his own.

The shepherd searched for hours

and wondered,

'Which way did he go?'

The naughty sheep stayed hiding
and he watched the sun sink low.

The night-time came:
the other sheep were safe
inside their fold.

But he could hear strange noises. Now he didn't feel so bold.

At last the shepherd found him. Both were pleased as pleased could be!

'Let's celebrate!' the shepherd called.

'My sheep's back safe with me!'

'And so remember,' Jesus said,
'if you feel lost and sad,

when you come safely home to God,
the angels all are glad.'

Other titles in this series from
Lion Children's Books

0 7459 4904 5

0 7459 4905 3